C Programming

It Was Never This Easy

Ganapati Das

Contents

Preface

In this concise and highly trimmed book, a brief history of the evolution of C language is presented. This is followed by the selection and installation of compiler. Although, MinGW compiler is used, the user is free to choose any other compiler of his/her choice. This chapter only gives a brief introduction of C to the beginners. Most of the complicated features(like Arrays, Pointers, Structures, Unions File handling etc.) of the language is avoided to keep the book simple.

Programming Languages

"A log with nine holes - old Turkish riddle for a man"

What are Programs?

Computer is incapable of doing anything for itself. Program tells the computer what to do. Definition of program by Stair, Ralph M., et al is as follows: *"A computer program is a sequence of instructions written to perform a specified task with a computer."* These programs can be written in various Computer Languages which is discussed in following sections.

What are Computer Languages?

Computers are made up of electronic components which understand only electric pulses which we often denote in terms of binary code with 0s and 1s. 0s mean OFF state and 1s mean ON. If instructions and data are to be given to the computer, it can be given in terms of 0s and 1s. Thus, such program written in 0s and 1s are known as Machine Language as the machine can easily understand it without translation. They are also known as low-level language. However, writing program in machine language is tedious and difficult to master by mortals like us. Although, early programmer did write some simple programs with machine language, it is almost impossible to write complex programs with machine language. This led to the development of Assembly Language. Assembly languages have the same structure and set of commands as machine languages, but they enable a programmer to use names instead of numbers.

Difficulty with machine and assembly language is that each type of CPU has its own machine language and assembly language, so an assembly language program written for one type of CPU will not run on another. Therefore modern programs are written with High-level Language. High-level Languages are languages written in English like language. These languages are beyond the capacity of the processor to understand. It needs to be translated in a machine equivalent language. This process of translation is carried out by special software called translators. Translators are discussed in next section. Some examples of high-level language are C/C++ language, Java, BASIC(Beginner's All Purpose Symbolic Instruction Code), FORTRAN(FORmula TRANslator), etc.

Translators

Let us start with an example. Suppose you visit China (and assume that you do not know Chinese) and you need to converse with a Chinese person who knows only Chinese. What would you do? Naturally, you would need the help of a translator who knows both English and Chinese. You can speak in English and the translator will translate it in Chinese. Chinese person will reply in Chinese which will be translated back to English by the translator. Similarly, a computer who can understand only machine language will not be able to understand an assembly language program and high-level language program. Therefore, we need a translator which will be able to translate our assembly or high-level languages also known as source code (source code is any collection of computer instructions written using some human-readable computer language) to machine language for the machine to understand and similarly convert the results back to assembly language or high-level language.

Types of Translators

Assembler

Assembly language is converted into executable machine code by a utility program referred to as an assembler; the conversion process is referred to as assembly, or assembling the code.

Interpreter

Consider the previous example of translator, where translator is interpreting every sentence as you speak in English.

Similarly and interpreter translate one line of code at a time. An interpreter converts the high-level language into machine level language but the interpreter will initially generate an intermediate code and then convert the high level language to machine level language. The process of interpretation can be depicted in Fig 1

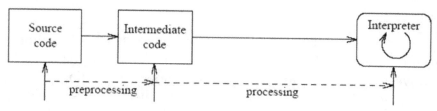

Figure 1: Interpretation

Compiler

Suppose on your visit to China, you need to listen to a live speech delivered in Chinese. In such situation, it may not be possible for the interpreter to translate each sentence at a time. Therefore, it would be better to translate the whole speech at a time to English. Similarly a compiler will translate the high level language input given by the user into the machine language, i.e. in the binary codes and executes the entire program at a time. Compiler also reports the list of errors that are caused during the process of execution and an autonomous executable file or object code is generated (Fig 2).

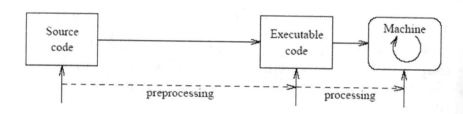

Figure 2: Compilation

Overview of C Language

"Sometimes to get to heaven you have to go through hell"

C is one of the most popular programming languages because it is a structured, high-level, machine independent language. C evolved from ALGOL (ALGOrithmic Language), BCPL(Basic Combined Programming Language) and B(another programming language based on BCPL) by Dennis Ritchie at Bell Laboratories in 1972. The language became more popular after publication of the book `The C Programming Language' by Brian Kerningham and Dennis Ritchie in 1978. Rapid growth of C led to the development of different versions of the language that were similar but often incompatible. To ensure that C language remains standard, American National Standards Institute (ANSI) approved a version of C in 1989 which is known as ANSI C. There are only 32 keywords in ANSI C.

Dennis Ritchie
1941-2011

Figure 3: Dannis Ritchie

Some of the reasons of the popularity of C is due to its many desirable qualities. It is a robust language with rich set of built-in functions and operators which can be used to write any complex program. Program written in C are efficient and fast. It is many time faster than BASIC (Beginner's All-purpose Symbolic

Instruction Code). It is highly portable, i.e., program written for one computer can be run on anther computer with little or no modification.

Compilers for C

Very first thing that you need to do, before writing a C program is to get a compiler (Discussed in earlier Chapter) which will convert the program that you write into executable that your computer will understand and run. Various Compilers are available for C language. We will use MinGW (Minimalist GNU for Windows), a native software port of the GCC (GNU Compiler Collection) produced by GNU Project.

Installing MinGW

MinGW is a free and open source product and can be downloaded from

$$http://sourceforge:net/projects/mingw/$$

Once downloaded, perform the following steps,

1. Copy the folder containing gcc into C: drive. In this case it is MinGW, which contain GCC(Fig 4).

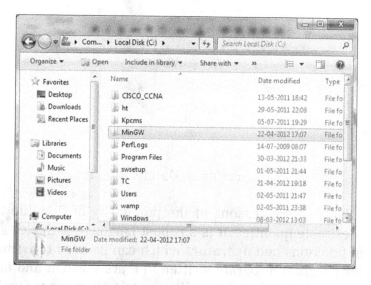

Figure 4: Copying MinGW folder

2. Add the path C :\MinGW\bin in the path variable. To add the path, perform the following steps:

(a) Right click on "My Computer" and select "Properties"(Fig 5).

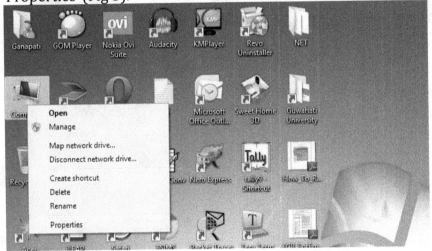

Figure 5: Adding to Path Variable Step 1

(b) Click on Advanced System Properties for windows 7 or Advanced tab for XP (Fig 6)

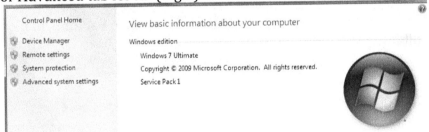

Figure 6: Adding to Path Variable Step 2

(c) On the Advanced tab, click on Environment Variables (Fig 7)

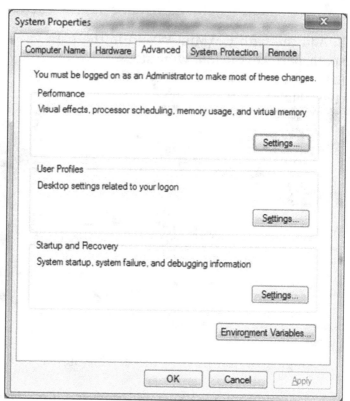

Figure 7: Adding to Path Variable Step 3

(d) Select Path from the System variable list and click on Edit button (Fig 8)

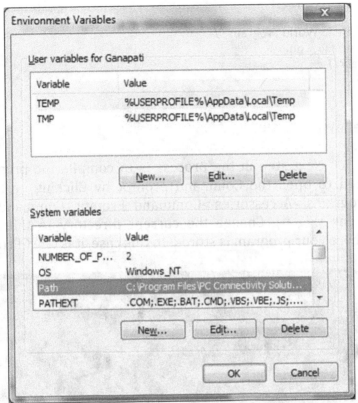

Figure 8: Adding to Path Variable Step 4

(e) Path variable already contains some value. Do not change anything but just add a semicolon(;) followed by the path C : \MinGW\bin and click OK.

Compiling C Program Using MinGW

In this section, we will learn to compile a C program. C program can be written using any text editor. Notepad program in Windows is a readily available text editors which you can used for creating C program. However, for bigger and more serious programming, I will recommend Notepad++.

We shall create a simple C Program for the purpose of demonstrating. Following listing (HelloWorld.c) created and saved into C : \CProg directory. You must have noticed by now that the filename had an extension .c. This is recommended for any C Program, although, it does not matter to some compiler.

```
/* Hello World program */
# include < stdio .h>
main ()
{
printf (" Hello World ");
}
```
HelloWorld.c

Next step in the process is to compile the program. We need to open the Command prompt by Clicking on Start->All Programs->Accessories->Command Prompt. Command Prompt opens (Fig 9). Change the current directory to the directory where your program is stored. In this case, it is C : \CProg.

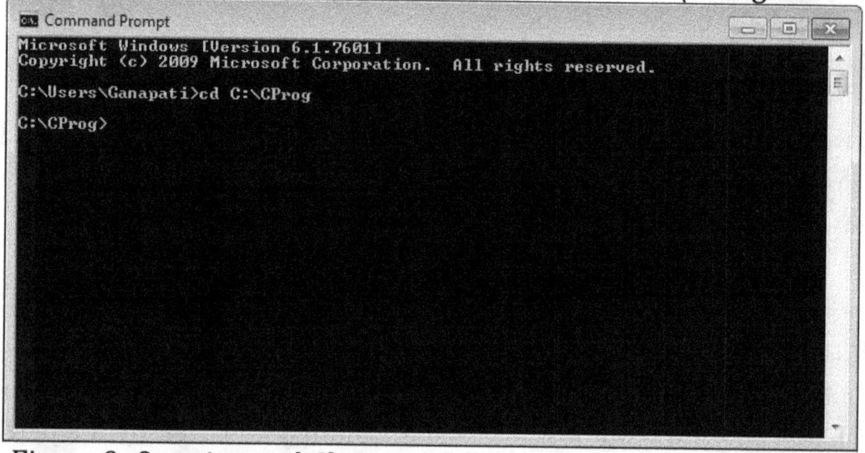

```
Command Prompt

Microsoft Windows [Version 6.1.7601]
Copyright (c) 2009 Microsoft Corporation.  All rights reserved.

C:\Users\Ganapati>cd C:\CProg

C:\CProg>
```

Figure 9: Opening and Changing Directory in Command Prompt

Compile your C program by using the command using the following syntax

gcc <filein.c >-o <fileout.exe >

where, filein.c is the name of the input file(e.g. HelloWorld.c) and fileout.exe is the name of the executable file to be produced. If we avoid it then a.out is produced by default. Thus, to compile HelloWorld.c, we write the command as follows

gcc HelloWorld.c -o HelloWorld.exe

We can run our program by simply writing the name of the executable file produced after compilation.

HelloWorld.exe

Entire process of compilation and execution of our first C program (HelloWorld) is shown in Figure 10.

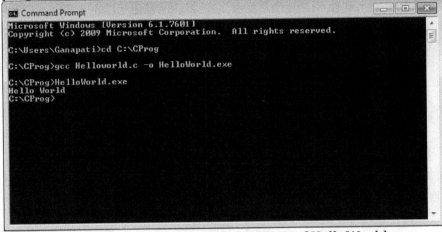

Figure 10: Compilation and Execution of HelloWorld.c

4.3 Basic Structure of C Program

C program can be viewed as a group of building blocks called functions. Function is designed to perform a specific task. To write a C Program, we first create functions and put them together. A C program can contain one or more sections as shown in Figure 11.

Document Section
Link Section
Definition Section
Global Declaration Section

main( ) Function Section
{
    Declaration Part
    Executable Part
}

Subprogram Section
    Function 1
    Function 2
    ...
    Function n

Figure 11: An overview of C program

The **Documentation Section** consist a set of comment lines giving the name of the program, the author and other details which the programmer will like to use later.

The **Link Section** provides instructions to the compiler to link functions in the system library.

The **Definition Section** defines all symbolic constants.

The **Global Declaration Section** declares all global variables and all user-defined functions. Global variable are variables used in more than one function.

Every C program must have on **main() function section**. This section contains two parts, *declaration part* and *executable part*. Declaration part declares the variable to be used in the executable part. Two parts must appear between the opening and closing curly braces.

The **Subprogram Section** contains all user-defined functions that are called in the main function.

All section except the main function section are optional and may be absent when they are not required.

Understanding the HelloWorld Program

We have seen the HelloWorld.c program in previous section. It consist of six lines of code which is still Greek to us. Let us have a close look at the program.

```
1 /* Hello World program */
2 # include < stdio .h>
3 main ( )
4 {
5       printf (" Hello World ");
6 }
HelloWorld.c
```

The statement in line 1 is delimited by /* and */ are known as comment lines. They only contains useful information about the program. They are not executable and anything between /* and */ are ignored by the compiler. C programs are divided into modules and functions. Some functions are written by us while many others are stored in the C library. These library functions are stored in different files known as header files. To include a header file we use the *#include* directive. We have used *printf* function which is in the header file *stdio.h*. Therefore the stdio.h header file is accessed in line 2. Line 3 contains the main( ) function. *main( )* function is a special function that tell the computer where the program starts. Every program have exactly one main function. The empty parenthesis immediately after the main indicates that main has no arguments. We will discuss arguments and parameter later. Opening braces at line 4 and closing braces in line 6 indicate the beginning and ending of the main function.

printf( ) in line 5 is the only executable statement. printf( ) function is a predefined function which is used to print output. Also note that printf( ) ends with a semicolon(;). Every statement in C must end with a semicolon(;) mark. printf( ) function also contains argument i.e. the string "Hello World", which is to be printed on the screen.

Character set of C

"To boldly go where no map has gone before"

We are familiar with natural language like English. In order to write English we need a set of characters like the 26 alphabets and numbers (0-9) and some special characters like period(.), comma(,), semicolon(;) etc. Similarly to write C program we need a set of characters which makes sense to the language. The Character in C are grouped into following categories.

1. Letters: All the alphabets A-Z (uppercase), a-z (lowercase)

2. Digits: All Decimal digits 0 . . . 9

3. Special Characters: Special characters supported in C are:

, comma
. period
; semicolon
: colon
? question mark
' apostrophe
\ quotation mark
! exclamation mark
j vertical bar
/ slash
\ backslash
~tilde
_underscore
$ dollar sign
% percentage sign
& ampersand
^ caret
* asterisk
- minus sign
+ plus sign
<opening angle bracket
>closing angle bracket

(left parenthesis
) right parenthesis
[left bracket
] right bracket
{ left braces
} right braces
number sign

4. White spaces: White spaces are also characters in C. White spaces supported in C are

Blank space
Horizontal tab
Carriage return
New line
Form feed

Tokens

In a passage of text, individual words and punctuation marks are called tokens. Similarly, in C program, the smallest individual units are known as C Tokens. C has six types of tokens. They are:

1. **Keywords**: Keyword serves as the basic building block of the program statements. Keywords have fixed meaning. Meaning cannot be changed. The list of keywords of ANSI C are as shown below.

break	case	char	const	continue
default	do	else	enum	extern
oat	for	goto	if	long
register	return	short	signed	sizeof
static	switch	typedef	union	unsigned
void	volatile	while		

2. **Identifier**: Identifier refers to name of variables, functions and arrays. These are user-defined names and consist of a sequence of letters and digits. While naming identifiers we must consider the following rules

(a) First character must be an alphabet.
(b) Must consist of only letters, digits or underscore

(c) Only 31 characters are significant
(d) Cannot use a keyword
(e) Must not contain white spaces

3. **Constants**: Constants in C refer to fixed values that do not change during the execution of a program. C supports several types of constants which can be broadly grouped as Numeric constants and Character constants.

4. **Strings**: Strings are set of character delimited by quotation marks. e.g. "ABC", "year", etc.

5. **Special Symbols**: Special symbols like [ ], ( ), etc.

6. **Operators**: Various operation like +, -, * etc.

Variables

A variable is a data name that may be used to store a data value. Unlike constants, variable may take different value at different time.

A variable name can be chosen by the programmer in a meaningful way so as to reflect its functions or nature in the program. Some examples are:
Average
height
Total
class_strength
While naming variables, we must keep in mind the rules for naming identifier discussed before.

Data Types

In computer science and computer programming, a data type or simply type is a classification identifying one of various types of data, such as real-valued, integer or Boolean, that determines the possible values for that type; the operations that can be done on values of that type; the meaning of the data; and the way values of that type can be stored. C Language is rich in data types. ANSI C supports three classes of data types

     1. **Primary (or fundamental) data types**
          Integer Types
          Floating Point Types
          Void Types
          Character Types
     2. **Derived data types**
          Arrays
          Functions
          Structures
          Pointers
     3. **User-defined data types**

Declaring Variables

After designing suitable variable names, we must declare them to the compiler. Declaration does two things

1. It tells compiler what the variable name is.
2. It specifies what type of data the variable will hold.

Syntax of declaring variables is a follows:

          data-type v1,v2,vn;

v1, v2, . vn are the name of the variables. For example, valid declarations are:

          int count;
          int number, total;
          double ratio;

int and *double* are the keywords to represent integer type and real type data values respectively.

Assigning Values to Variables

Values can be assigned to the variable using assignment (=) operator. Syntax for assigning values to the variable is as follows:

          variable name = constant;

Examples:

          number = 100;
          intial values = 0;

yes = 'x';

It is possible to assign variable at the time of declaration. For doing so, we must use the following syntax

data-type variable name = constant;

For example:

int _nal = 100;
char yes = 'x';
double balance = 75.86;

Operators and Expressions

"When the world lets me down, I'll paint a smile."

An operator is a symbols that tells the computer to perform certain mathematical or logical manipulations. Operators are used in programs to manipulate data and variables. C supports a rich set of built-in operators. C operators can be classified into number of categories. They include:
1. Arithmetic Operators
2. Relational Operators
3. Logical Operators
4. Assignment Operators
5. Increment and Decrement Operators
6. Conditional Operators
7. Bitwise Operators
8. Special Operators

In this book, we shall limit our scope to the first five categories only. It will be discussed in the subsequent sections.

An expression is a sequence of operands and operators that reduces to a single value. For example: 10+15 is an expression whose value is 25.

Arithmetic Operators

C provides all basic arithmetic operators. They are listed in Table 4.1.

+ Addition or unary plus
- Subtraction or unary minus
* Multiplication
/ Division
% Modulo division

Table 1: Arithmetic Operators

Integer Arithmetic

When both the operands in a single arithmetic expression are integer, the expression is called integer expression, and the operation is called integer arithmetic. Let us understand the arithmetic operators using a program. In the following program, we have declared two integers **a** and **b** in line 5. In line 6, **a** is assigned a value of 14. Similarly, in line 7, **b** gets a value of 4. Line 8 to 12 contains the print statements displaying the results of the operations. If you pay attention to the print statements, you will also notice two strange looking character, `%d' and `\n'. The '%'s tell printf where the variables should be placed. '%d' means the input should be an integer number, '%f' means it should be a floating or real number. It is important to use the appropriate %.

C also supports some special backlash character constants that are used in output functions. '\n' in the printf( ) function stands for a new line character. A new line will be created whenever printf( ) encounters '\n'. Hence output is separated in different lines.

```
1 /* Arithmetic Operators : Real Arithmetic */
2 # include < stdio .h>
3 main ()
4 {
5        int a, b;
6        a = 14;
7        b = 4;
8        printf ("a + b = %d \n",a+b);
9        printf ("a - b = %d \n",a-b);
10       printf ("a * b = %d \n",a*b);
11       printf ("a / b = %d \n",a/b);
12       printf ("a % b = %d \n",a%b);
13 }
ArithmeticOperators.c
```

Output

a + b = 18
a - b = 10
a * b = 56
a / b = 3
a % b = 2

If you see the output of the above program, you will notice that the results of addition, subtraction and multiplication are correctly displayed as 18, 10 and 56 respectively. But the result of division shows only 3 whereas you must have expected it to show as 3.5. This is because result of the integer arithmetic is always an integer. Hence, decimal part is truncated. Another operator denoted as '%' is known as modulo division returns the remainder of division.

Real Arithmetic

When both the operands in a single arithmetic expression are real, the operation is called real arithmetic.

Mixed-mode Arithmetic

When one of the operand is real and the other is integer, the expression is called a mixed-mode arithmetic expression. In such cases, the result is always a real number which is depicted in following listing.

```
1 /* Arithmetic Operators : Mixed - mode Arithmetic */
2 # include < stdio .h>
3 main ()
4 {
5       float a;
6       int b;
7       a = 15;
8       b = 10;
9       printf ("a / b = %f \n",a/b);
10 }
ArithmeticOperatorsMixedmode.c
```

Output
a / b = 1.500000

Relational Operators

We often need to compare two quantities. These comparisons can be done with the help of relational operators.

The value of the relational operator is either one or zero. C supports six relational operators as shown in Table 2.

< is less than
_ is less than or equal to
> is greater than
_ is greater than or equal to
== is equal to
! = is not equal to

Table 2: Relational Operators

Logical Operators

In addition to the relational operators, C has three logical operators.

&& meaning logical AND
|| meaning logical OR
! meaning logical NOT

Assignment Operators

Assignment operators are used to assign the result of an expression to a variable. We have already seen and used assignment operator (=) in our previous program while assigning values to the variables.

Increment and Decrement Operators

C allow two very useful operators called increment and decrement operators:

++ and --

The operator ++ adds 1 to the operand, while -- subtracts 1. Both are unary operators and takes the following forms

m++ or ++m
m-- or –m

Managing Input Output Operations

"Life is like a novel. You can guess what will happen on the next chapter, but you will not know until youre there."

We have already explored the *printf( )* function in our previous listings. While *printf( )* is used for display output to the user, we have the *scanf( )* function which is used for taking input from the user.

Taking Input from the User

We can use the *scanf( )* functions for taking formatted input from the user. The general form of the *scanf( )* function is as follows:

scanf(\Control string", arg1, arg2,. . . argn);

The control string specifies the field format in which the data is to be entered and the arg1, arg2, . . . argn specifies the variable(address locations) where the data is stored. Control string is also known as format string contains the field specification consisting of the conversion character %, a data type character. In addition, it may also contain blank space, tab, or newlines. Commonly used format code for *printf( )* and *scanf( )* are shown in Table 3.

%c Character
%d Integer
%f Floating point value

Table 3: Format Code in C

Let us understand the taking of input with the help of an example. Following program takes an integer input from the user using *scanf( )* function and then displays the same to the user using the *printf( )* function.

```
1 # include < stdio .h>
2 main ()
3 {
4        int num ;
```

```
5        printf (" Enter a number :");
6        scanf ("%d" ,&num);
7        printf ("The number you have entered is %d", num
);

8 }
```
Input.c

Output:
Enter a number:45
The number you have entered is 45

In the above example, a variable num is declared in line 4. Line 5 includes a *printf( )* statement which is used for displaying the string "Enter a number:". Line 6 contains the *scanf( )* function with the format specifier %d followed by the variable **&num**. %d tells the compiler that input should be converted to an integer and **&num** says that the value should be stored at the address **num. &** before **num** is the address of operator.

Displaying Output to the User

We have already used the *printf( )* statement several times in our previous listing. In this section, we will try to understand the *printf( )* in more detail. The general form of the *printf( )* is as follow:

printf(\Control string" , arg1, arg2,..., argn);

Control string consist of three types of items:

1. Characters that will be printed on the screen as they appear.

2. Format specifications that define the output format for display of each item.

3. Escape sequence characters such as \n, \t, and \b.

The following program demonstrates some variation of *printf( )* function.

```
1 # include < stdio .h>
2 main ()
3 {
```

```
4       int num = 10;
5       printf (" Programming in C");
6       printf (" ");
7       printf ("%d", 24 );
8       printf ("\n");
9       printf (" Number = %d\n", num );
10      printf ("Hope , you could understand printf ()");
11 }
```
Output.c

Output:
Programming in C 24
Number = 10
Hope, you could understand printf( )

In the above program, line 5 prints the string "Programming in C". There is no newline character and thus the cursor remains after 'C'. Next *printf( )* statement in line 6 prints blank space immediately after 'C'. Printf statement in line 7 contains a format specifier for printing an integer, and thus prints the argument 24 after the blank space. Newline character in line 8 takes the cursor to the next line and therefore the printf statement in line 9 prints its output in the next line. You must have also noticed the newline character in line 9, which cause the next printf statement to be printed on the next line.

Let us now write a simple program in C to calculate the sum of two integer.

```
1 /* Add two integer number by taking input from the
user */
2 # include < stdio .h>
3 main ()
4 {
5       int num1 , num2 , result ;
6       printf (" Enter the first number :");
7       scanf ("%d" ,& num1 );
8       printf (" Enter the second number :");
9       scanf ("%d" ,& num2 );
```

```
10      result = num1 + num2 ;
11      printf ("The sum is %d", result );
12 }
```
AddInteger.c

Output:
Enter the first number :3
Enter the second number :4
The sum is 7

Decision Making and Branching

"If you're going through hell, keep going"

Until now, C program in the example had a set of statements which was executing in a sequence. But, at times there are situations when we have to change the order of execution based on some condition or repeat a group of statements until certain specified conditions are met. Decision control instruction can be implemented in C using:

The if statement
The if . . . else statement
The Conditional Operators
switch statement
goto statement

if Statement

C uses the keyword **if** to implement the decision control instruction. The general form of if statement looks like this:

```
if (test expression)

{

        statement-block;

}

statement-x;
```

The 'statement-block' may be a single statement or a group of statements. If the text-expression is true, the statement-block will be executed; otherwise statement-block will skipped and the execution will jump to the statement-x. However, if condition is true, then both the statement-block and statement-x will be executed. Here is a simple program, which demonstrates the use of if and the relational operators.

```
1 /* Demonstration of if statement */
2 # include < stdio .h>
3 main ( )
4 {
5       int num ;
6       printf ( " Enter a number less than 10 " ) ;
7       scanf ( "%d", &num ) ;
8       if ( num <= 10 )
9       {
10              printf ( " What an obedient servant you are
!" ) ;
11      }
12 }
```
simpleif.c

Output:
Enter a number less than 10 6
What an obedient servant you are !
Enter a number less than 10 15

On execution of this program, if you type a number less than or equal to 10 (as in the first case number was 6), you get a message on the screen through printf( ). If you type some other number the program doesn't do anything (in the second case when 15 was entered).

if. . . else Statement

The **if** statement by itself will execute a single statement, or a block of statements, when the expression following if evaluates to true. It does nothing when the expression evaluates to false. To execute one group of statements if the expression evaluates to true and another group of statements if the expression evaluates to false, we can make use of **if . . . else** statement. The general form is:

```
if (test expression)
{
        true-statement-block;
}
```

```
else
{
        false-statement-block;
}
statement-x;
```

If the test expression is true, then the *true-statement-block* immediately following **if** will be executed; otherwise, *false-statement-block* will be executed after the **else** keyword. In this case either *true-statement-block* or *false-statement-block* will be executed but not both. *statement-x* will always be executed. Example of **if. . . else** statement is demonstrated with the following example:

In a company an employee is paid as under: If his basic salary is less than $. 1500, then HRA = 10% of basic salary and DA = 90% of basic salary. If his salary is either equal to or above $1500, then HRA = $500 and DA = 98% of basic salary. If the employee's salary is input through the keyboard, the program should find his gross salary.

```
1 /* Calculation of gross salary */
2 # include < stdio .h>
3 main ( )
4 {
5        float bs , gs , da , hra ;
6        printf ( " Enter basic salary " ) ;
7        scanf ( "%f", &bs ) ;
8        if ( bs < 1500 )
9        {
10               ra = bs * 10 / 100 ;
11               da = bs * 90 / 100 ;
12       }
13       else
14       {
15               hra = 500 ;
16               da = bs * 98 / 100 ;
17       }
18       gs = bs + hra + da ;
```

```
19      printf ( " gross salary = Rs. %f", gs ) ;
20 }
```
ifelse.c

Output:
Enter basic salary 1200
gross salary = Rs. 2400.000000

Nesting of if

It is perfectly all right if we write an entire if-else construct within either the body of the if statement or the body of an else statement. This is called 'nesting'of **ifs**. This is shown in the following program. You will see that each time a **if-else** construct is nested within another **if-else** construct, it is also indented to add clarity to the program. If not indented properly, you would end up writing programs which nobody (you included) can understand easily at a later date.

```
1 /* Nested if - else */
2 # include < stdio .h>
3 main ()
4 {
5       int i ;
6       printf (" Enter either 1 or 2 ");
7       scanf ("%d", &i) ;
8       if(i == 1)
9               printf (" You are a real C programmer ");
10      else
11      {
12              if(i == 2)
13      printf ("You love to learn C");
14      else
15      printf ("How about Java !");
16      }
17 }
```
nestingif.c

Output:

Enter either 1 or 2 1
You are a real C programmer
Enter either 1 or 2 2
You love to learn C
Enter either 1 or 2 6
How about Java !

The Conditional Operator

C language has an unusual operator for making two way decisions. The conditional operator is a combination of ? and : are sometimes called ternary operators since they take three arguments. In fact, they form a kind of foreshortened if-then-else.

The general form is,

conditional expression ? expression1 : expression2;

The Conditional expression is evaluated first and if the result is nonzero, expression1 is executed otherwise expression2 is executed. For example:

```
if (x<0)
{
        ag = 0;
}
else
{
        ag = 1;
}
```

can be written as

```
ag = (x <0) ? 0 : 1;
```

Switch Statement

C has a built-in multiway decision statement known as **switch** or more correctly a **switch-case-default**, since these three keywords go together to make up the control statement. The general form is shown below:

```
switch(integer expression)
{
        case value-1:
```

```
                block-1
                break;
                case value-2:
                block-2
                break;
                . . . . . .
                . . . . . .
                default:
                default-block;
                break;
        }
        statement-x
```

The expression is an integer expression or characters. value-1, value-2, ... are constant or constant expressions and are known as case labels. Each of these values should be unique within a switch statement. block-1, block-2, ... are statement lists and may contain zero or more statements. There is no need to put braces around these blocks.

When the switch is executed, the value of the expression is successfully compared against the value-1, value-2,. ... If a case found whose value matches with the value of expression, then the block of statements that follows the case are executed. If none of the case label matches then the default block is executed.

The break statement at the end of each block tells the compiler of the end of block and causes it to exit out of the switch. Use of switch is demonstrated in the following listing.

```
1 /* Demo of Switch -case - default */
2 # include < stdio .h>
3 main ( )
4 {
5        int i;
6        intf (" Enter an integer :");
7        scanf ("%d", &i);
8        switch ( i )
9        {
```

```c
10          case 1 :
11                  printf ( "I am in case 1 \n" ) ;
12                  break ;
13          case 2 :
14                  printf ( "I am in case 2 \n" ) ;
15                  break ;
16          case 3 :
17                  printf ( "I am in case 3 \n" ) ;
18                  break ;
19          default :
20                  printf ( "I am in default \n" ) ;
21      }
22 }
```
switch.c

Output:
Enter an integer:1
I am in case 1

Enter an integer:2
I am in case 2

Enter an integer:3
I am in case 3

Enter an integer:5
I am in default

Decision Making and Looping

"When the world lets me down, I'll paint a smile".

Often in programming, we need to execute a set of statements repetitively. This can be achieved by placing the statement(s) to be repeated inside a loop statement. Each process of repetition is also called as *iteration of the loop*. There are three methods by way of which we can repeat a part of a program. They are:

- Using a *while* statement.
- Using a *for* statement.
- Using a *do-while* statement.

The While Statement

The simplest of all the looping structure in C is the while statement. The basic format of the while statement is:

```
while (test condition)
{
body of the loop
}
```

The test condition is evaluated and if the condition is true then the body of the loop is executed. After execution of the body, the condition is once again evaluated and if it is true, the body of the loop is executed once again. The process is repeated until the test condition finally becomes false. On exit, the program continues with the statement immediately after the body of the loop. The following program finds the sum of first ten integer using a while loop.

```
1 # include < stdio .h>
2 main ( )
3 {
4       int i, sum ;
5       i=1;
6       sum =0;
7       while ( i <= 10)
```

```
8      {
9              sum = sum + i;
10             i++; // Incrementing is very important
11     }
12     printf ( " Sum of the first ten integer is %d", sum );
13 }
```
suminteger.c

Output:
Sum of the first ten integer is 55

Following program also uses a while loop to find the simple interest 3 times.

```
1 /* Calculation of simple interest for 3 sets of p, n and r */
2 # include < stdio .h>
3 main ( )
4 {
5        int p, n, count ;
6        float r, si ;
7        count = 1 ;
8        while ( count <= 3 )
9        {
10              printf ( "\ nEnter values of p, n and r " ) ;
11              scanf ( "%d %d %f", &p, &n, &r ) ;
12              si = p *n * r / 100 ;
13              printf ( " Simple interest = Rs. %f", si ) ;
14              count = count +1;
15      }
16 }
```
simpleinterest.c

Output:
Enter values of p, n and r 5000 8 12.5
Simple interest = Rs. 5000.000000
Enter values of p, n and r 5000 8 13.0
Simple interest = Rs. 5200.000000
Enter values of p, n and r 10000 5 12.0

Simple interest = Rs. 6000.000000

The For Statement

For loop is one of the most popular loop that provides a more concise loop control structure. The general form of the for loop is

for (initialization ; test-condition ; increment)
{
      body of the loop
}

The execution of the for loop is as follows:
1. Setting a loop counter to an initial value.
2. Testing the loop counter with the test-condition to determine whether its value has reached the number of repetitions desired. If the condition is true then the body of the loop is executed. Otherwise, execution continues with the statement that immediately follows the loop.
3. Once the body of the loop is executed, the control is transferred back to the **for** statement. Now the counter is incremented using the increment mentioned and tested against the test-condition once again. If the condition still holds true, then the body of the loop is executed again otherwise it exits the loop.

The following program uses the for loop to print the sum of the first ten positive integer.

```
1 /* Sum of First Ten Positive Integer using For loop */
2 # include < stdio .h>
3 main ()
4 {
5        int i;
6        int sum =0;
7        for ( i=1 ; i <= 10; i++)
8        {
9                sum = sum + i;
10       }
```

```
    11      printf ("The sum of First Ten Positive Integer is
%d", sum );
    12 }
```
sumintegerfor.c

Output:

The sum of First Ten Positive Integer is 55

In the above program, you must have noticed that variable i was not initialized in the declaration. This is because **i** was initialized within the **for** statement. Moreover, **i** is not incremented within the loop (as in the case of while loop) because the increment operation in the **for** statement takes care of it.

The Do Statement

C provides another loop structure similar to the while loop called as do loop or do-while loop. The only difference is where the test condition is evaluated. The while tests the condition before executing any of the statements within the while loop. As against this, the do-while tests the condition after having executed the statements within the loop. The general form of the loop is:

```
    do
    {
            body of the loop
    }
    while (test-condition)
```

In the case of do-while, it would execute the body of the loop at least once, even if the condition fails for the first time.

Nesting of Loops

As in the case of branching statements (e.g. if), the loops can also be nested. When loops are nested, then the innermost loop iterates completely for each iteration of the outer loops. Following program uses a nested for loop to print a pattern. In this case a for loop is nested inside another for loop. For each iteration of the outer for loop (i.e. with counter i), the inner for loop (i.e. with counter j) is iterated completely. The inner loop prints (*) character on each iteration while the outer loop prints a newline character in each iteration.

```
1 /* Nesting of for Loop */
2 # include < stdio .h>
3 main ()
4 {
5      int i, j;
6      for ( i = 1 ; i <= 5; i++)
7      {
8              for ( j =1 ; j <= i; j++)
9              {
10                     printf ("*");
11             }
12             printf ("\n");
13     }
14 }
```

nestingloop.c

Output:
```
*
**
***
****
*****
```

Jumps in the Loop

Sometime when executing a loop, it becomes desirable to skip a part of the loop or to leave the loop as soon as a certain condition occurs. This can be accomplished in C using the following statements:

1. *break* Statement
2. *continue* Statement

break Statement

We often come across situations where we want to jump out of a loop instantly, without waiting to get back to the conditional test. The keyword break allows us to do this. When break is encountered inside any loop, control automatically passes to the first statement after the loop. A break is usually associated with an if. As an example, let's consider the following program to find whether a particular number is prime or not.

```
1 # include < stdio .h>
2 main ()
3 {
4       int num , i ;
5       printf ( " Enter a number " ) ;
6       scanf ( "%d", &num ) ;
7       i = 2 ;
8       while ( i <= num - 1 )
9       {
10              if ( num % i == 0 )
11              {
12                      printf ( " Not a prime number " ) ;
13                      break ;
14              }
15              i++ ;
16      }
17      if ( i == num )
18              printf ( " Prime number " ) ;
19 }
break.c
```

Output:
Enter a number 5
Prime number
Enter a number 6
Not a prime number

In this program the moment num % i turns out to be zero, (i.e. num is exactly divisible by i) the message "Not a prime number" is printed and the control breaks out of the while loop.

continue Statement

In some programming situations we want to take the control to the beginning of the loop, bypassing the statements inside the loop, which have not yet been executed. The keyword *continue* allows us to do this. When *continue* is encountered inside any loop, control automatically passes to the beginning of the loop.

Let us see this with the following program.

```
1 # include < stdio .h>
2 main ()
3 {
4        int i;
5        for ( i = 1 ; i <= 10 ; i++)
6        {
7                if ( i == 5)
8                {
9                        continue ;
10               }
11               printf ("%d \n", i);
12       }
13 }
continue.c
```

Output:
1
2
3
4
6
7
8
9
10

As you can see in the output that number 5 is not printed. This is due to the fact that when i was equal to 5, the control moved to the beginning of the loop hence the print statement which was after it was not executed once.